Best Practices for the
Safe Use of Glutaraldehyde in Health Care

U.S. Department of Labor

Occupational Safety and Health Administration

OSHA 3258-08N
2006

Contents

Introduction

This document describes best practices for the safe use of glutaraldehyde in health care facilities. Glutaraldehyde is used widely as a cold sterilant to disinfect a variety of heat-sensitive instruments, such as endoscopes, bronchoscopes, and dialysis equipment (NIOSH, 2001). In addition, health care employees may be exposed to glutaraldehyde in its uses as a hardener in x-ray developing and as a tissue fixative in histology and pathology labs.

Glutaraldehyde's properties as a chemical sterilant were initially recognized in the early 1960s as the health care industry searched for a safer alternative to formaldehyde, which is regulated by OSHA as a carcinogen (29 CFR 1910.1048). In the years since its introduction as a disinfectant/sterilant, glutaraldehyde has been linked with a variety of health effects – ranging from mild to severe – including asthma, breathing difficulties, respiratory irritation, and skin rashes (Pryor, 1984; Crandall, 1987).

The purpose of this document is to provide information that can be used by health care employers and employees to understand and control exposures to glutaraldehyde. This document describes engineering controls, work practices, and facility design considerations that will help reduce employee exposure to glutaraldehyde. This document also includes recommendations for personal protective equipment, employee training, exposure monitoring, disposal practices, and spill and cleanup procedures. The use of alternatives to glutaraldehyde is also addressed.

Note: The term "health care facilities" is intended to encompass the broad range of health care facility types and sizes, including hospitals, clinics, freestanding surgical centers, physician offices, and dental clinics, as well as nursing homes and other residential health care facilities.

Summary of Health Effects

The most serious adverse health effect documented among employees exposed to glutaraldehyde vapor is occupational asthma, a chronic condition characterized by bronchial hyperre-sponsiveness. Reactions can be either immediate or delayed, with a latent period ranging from a few weeks to several years from the onset of exposure. Human studies on the effects of glu-taraldehyde exposure consist of many case reports in the published literature, some identified by both American and British health surveillance systems, and symptom surveys of American health care employees, all of which document an association between exposure to glutaraldehyde and the development of asthma. (Gannon et al., 1995; Rosenman et al., 1997; Keynes et al., 1996; Di Stefano et al., 1999).

In addition, a few cross-sectional studies also show that an increased prevalence of irritant symptoms, including itching of the eyes with increased lacrimation (tearing), and rhinitis, is reported by health care employees who are exposed to short-term (15-minute) concentrations well below 0.2 parts-per-million (ppm) in air, predominantly in the range of about 0.005 to 0.050 ppm (Norback, 1988; Pisaniello et al., 1995).

In addition to causing respiratory effects, glutaraldehyde acts as a contact allergen, giving rise to contact dermatitis, usually on the hands but occasionally on the face. Skin sensitization from contact with glutaraldehyde has been documented in endoscopy nurses, dental assistants, x-ray technicians, hospital maintenance and cleaning staff, and funeral service employees (Marzulli and Maibach, 1974; Fowler, 1989; Nethercott et al., 1988; Maibach and Prystowsky, 1977; Nethercott and Holness, 1988; Ballantyne and Berman, 1984; Waters et al., 2003). Individuals who have become sensitized to glutaraldehyde can develop dermatitis after contacting solutions containing as little as 0.1 percent glutaralde-hyde. In contrast, simple skin irritation typically occurs on contact with solutions containing more than 2 percent glutaralde-hyde (HSE, 1997). In one study of health care employees who had developed allergic contact dermatitis from glutaraldehyde, ten employees who were followed for six months after initial diagnosis continued to have persistent hand eczema, although five of these employees had left their jobs because of this health problem (Nethercott et al., 1988).

Occupational Exposure Limits for Glutaraldehyde

The Federal Occupational Safety and Health Administration (OSHA) does not have a Permissible Exposure Limit for glutaraldehyde. The National Institute for Occupational Safety and Health (NIOSH) established a Recommended Exposure Limit (REL) of 0.2 ppm in 1989 (http://www.cdc.gov/niosh/npg/npgd0301.html). Other organizations that have occupational exposure limits include the American Conference of Governmental Industrial Hygienists (ACGIH), which currently recommends a Threshold Limit Value (TLV) of 0.05 ppm in air, measured as a ceiling concentration, and the United Kingdom Health and Safety Executive which also has established a 0.05 ppm Workplace Exposure Limit (WEL) averaged over both 8 hours and 15 minutes.

The occupational exposure limits discussed above were current at the time this document was published. However, it is essential that health care personnel keep informed of current Federal, state, and local regulations applicable to glutaraldehyde, as well as with professional guidelines.

GLUTARALDEHYDE USE AS A HIGH-LEVEL DISINFECTANT

Primary Sources of Glutaraldehyde Exposure

Glutaraldehyde-based agents are used to disinfect medical equipment that cannot be subjected to steam sterilization, specifically heat-sensitive, lensed devices typically requiring high-level disinfection between patient uses (ANSI/AAMI, 1996). Glutaraldehyde-based products may be used in a variety of locations within a facility, such as surgery, endoscopy, and respiratory therapy. Trade names of glutaraldehyde-based products include, but are not limited to, Cidex®, Sonacide®, Sporicidin®, Hospex®, and Omnicide® (NIOSH, 2001).

Definitions:

Sterilant: Physical or chemical agent(s) or process which completely eliminates or destroys all forms of life, particularly microorganisms.

Disinfectant: An agent that destroys pathogens by physical or chemical means. Disinfection processes do not ensure the same margin of safety associated with sterilization processes and can vary in their extent of microorganism elimination. This variation leads to subcategories, the first of which is high-level disinfection.

High-Level Disinfection: A process utilizing a sterilant under less than sterilizing conditions. The process kills all forms of microbial life except for large numbers of bacterial spores.

Disinfection activities range from simple soaking of small instruments to automated processing of complex lensed instruments, such as endoscopes. Exposure to glutaraldehyde as a high-level disinfectant occurs primarily during the following activities:

- activating and pouring glutaraldehyde solution into or out of a cleaning container system (e.g., soaking basin in manual disinfecting operations and reservoir in automated processors);
- opening the cleaning container system to immerse instruments to be disinfected;
- agitating glutaraldehyde solution;
- handling of soaked instruments;
- removing instruments from the container system;
- rinsing the channels of instruments containing residual glutaraldehyde solution;
- flushing out instrument parts with a syringe;
- drying instrument interiors with compressed air;
- disposing of "spent" glutaraldehyde solutions to the sanitary sewer;
- performing maintenance procedures, such as filter or hose changes on automated processors that have not been pre-rinsed with water.

Measurements of health care employee exposure to glutaraldehyde vapor during high-level disinfection have been reported to range from none detected to 0.20 ppm or greater (Naidu et al., 1995; Pisaniello et al., 1997). NIOSH has documented levels as high as 0.5 ppm (NIOSH, 1985); 0.48 ppm (NIOSH, 1987); and 0.08 ppm (NIOSH, 1991) during disinfection procedures at health care facilities. A recent study (Waters et al., 2003) documented exposures of up to 0.15 ppm in endoscopy disinfection. Exposure levels will vary depending on a number of factors such as the concentration of the glutaraldehyde solution, type of process (manual versus automatic), ventilation conditions, site-specific factors, as well as the duration of the sampling period (e.g., peak, 15-minute short-term, or full task duration).

Manual operations with inadequate or ineffective controls result in higher exposures. Pisaniello et al. (1997) reported on exposures in operating theaters and endoscopy areas with and without local exhaust ventilation (LEV). In endoscopy units, the mean geometric exposure of 14 samples without LEV was 0.093 ppm, and 0.022 ppm with LEV. Figure 1 presents some exposure data for specific operations with and without exposure controls.

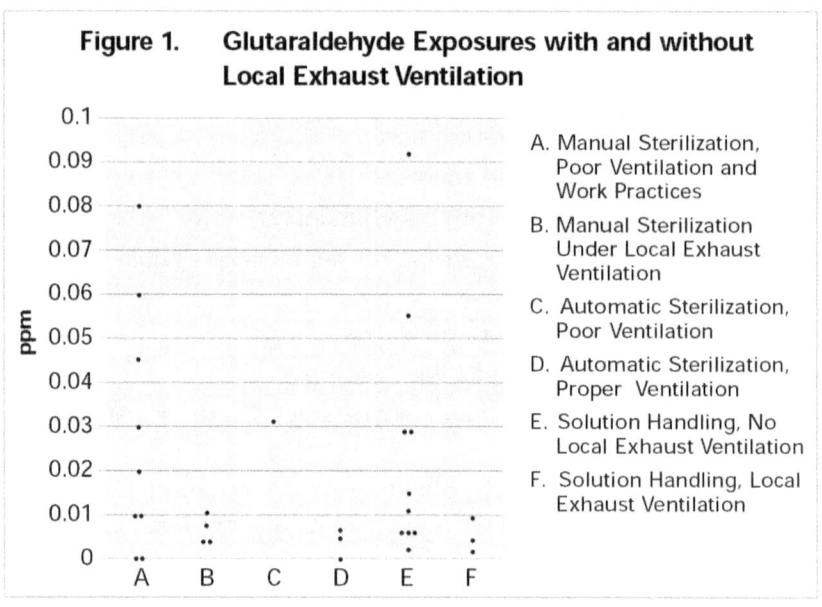

Figure 1.   Glutaraldehyde Exposures with and without Local Exhaust Ventilation

A. Manual Sterilization, Poor Ventilation and Work Practices

B. Manual Sterilization Under Local Exhaust Ventilation

C. Automatic Sterilization, Poor Ventilation

D. Automatic Sterilization, Proper Ventilation

E. Solution Handling, No Local Exhaust Ventilation

F. Solution Handling, Local Exhaust Ventilation

Sources: NIOSH, 1991; NJDOHSS, 1998; Naidu et al., 1995. All exposures are personal breathing zone samples.

Recommended Exposure Controls

A variety of engineering controls, facility design considerations, and work practices are available to minimize exposure to glutaraldehyde during its use as a disinfectant and sterilant. In good industrial hygiene practice such methods are to be used to control employee exposure, and if they prove to be insufficient to protect employees, respirators and other personal protective equipment are to be used. Employees required by their employer to wear respirators must receive training and a medical evaluation to determine their fitness to use the equipment. Fit testing of the respirator is also required. For details on fit testing and other requirements for employee use of respirators see OSHA's Respiratory Protection standard (29 CFR 1910.134). Employees whose employers do not require them to wear respirators but who choose to do so must obtain certain information concerning the safe use of respirators (Appendix D to Part 1910.134). Respirators protect only the user, and others in the area may be overexposed to glutaraldehyde vapor if it is not adequately controlled at the source of the release.

Other forms of personal protective equipment (PPE), such as gloves, safety eyewear, and isolation gowns, lab coats, or aprons (plus sleeve protectors) should be worn and may be required whenever there is the potential for skin or eye contact with glutaraldehyde. See the following OSHA standards: Personal Protective Equipment, General Requirements (29 CFR 1910.132); Eye and Face Protection (29 CFR 1910.133); Respiratory Protection (29 CFR 1910.134) and Hand Protection (29 CFR 1910.138), and ANSI/AAMI, 1996. Such PPE should always be used *in combination* with effective engineering controls.

Studies have documented the effectiveness of controls in reducing exposure to gluataraldehyde in disinfecting. Butt et al. (1999) documented exposures during sterilization and mixing over a 5-month period, while changes to ventilation, equipment and work practices were made. During this time, exposures to glutaraldehyde during mixing decreased from a high of 0.96 ppm down to 0.04 ppm. The authors indicated that the changes that appeared to have the most impact on reducing mixing exposures were the addition of a waste pump and new filters in the hood.

This section describes recommended engineering controls and work practices to reduce glutaraldehyde exposures to safe levels during disinfection activities. This section also summarizes the most recent information concerning possible substitutes for glutaraldehyde. Employers should consider whether for a particular use of glutaraldehyde there is an effective substitute that has reduced risks to employees.

See *General Recommendations* section of this publication at page 23 for additional information on the selection and use of personal protective equipment, employee information and training, exposure monitoring, disposal of glutaraldehyde solutions, and spill and cleanup procedures applicable to the use of glutaraldehyde as a high-level disinfectant.

Engineering Controls

The goal of engineering controls is to keep glutaraldehyde vapor from entering the workroom and the employee's breathing zone by containing and removing it at the source of release. As described above, the primary sources of employee exposure to glutaraldehyde during disinfection/sterilant activities include pouring glutaraldehyde solutions into container systems, opening soaking basins or reservoirs, and handling instruments containing residual glutaraldehyde. Engineering controls tailored for these exposure sources include ventilation, both general exhaust ventilation and local exhaust systems (such as laboratory chemical hoods), process automation, and isolation (e.g., basins with tight-fitting covers, dedicated centralized storage and use areas).

General Room Ventilation
The American National Standards Institute, Inc., in collaboration with the Association for the Advancement of Medical Instrumentation, recommends that rooms where glutaraldehyde disinfection/sterilization is performed be large enough to ensure adequate dilution of vapor and have a *minimum air exchange rate of 10 air exchanges per hour* (ANSI/AAMI, 1996). Some agencies recommend even higher air exchange rates, e.g., 15 air exchanges per

hour, to ensure dilution of vapor. There are no national standards that apply specifically to glutaraldehyde usage areas; however, local codes may apply. The air exchange rate recommended by ANSI/ AAMI is consistent with the American Institute of Architects' guidelines for health care facilities (ANSI/AAMI, 1996).

Local Exhaust Ventilation

ANSI/AAMI ST58 recommends that local exhaust ventilation <u>also</u> be installed at the point of release of glutaraldehyde vapors. The health care facility must ensure that the ventilation system is operating properly and is not obstructed or disturbed by drafts from sources such as fans, supply air diffusers, open windows and doors, and heavily traveled aisles.

Local exhaust ventilation located at the level of vapor discharge is the preferred method of reducing glutaraldehyde vapor concentrations because it captures and removes vapor at the source before it can escape into the general work environment. Local exhaust ventilation systems for glutaraldehyde-based activities may include a local exhaust hood (such as a laboratory fume hood) and the associated ductwork and fan; or, a self-contained, freestanding, recirculating exhaust ventilation system (i.e., ductless fume hood).

Local Exhaust Hood

The purpose of a local exhaust hood is to capture glutaraldehyde vapor during processing and conduct it into the exhaust system (via the hood). The capture and control of glutaraldehyde vapor is achieved by the inward airflow created by the exhaust hood. The minimum hood-induced air velocity necessary to capture and convey glutaraldehyde vapor into the hood is called the "capture velocity." Pryor (1984) recommends a minimum capture velocity of at least 100 feet per minute to prevent exposure to glutaraldehyde vapor.

The average velocity of the air drawn through the face (opening) of the hood is called the "face velocity." The face velocity of a hood greatly influences the containment efficiency of the hood (i.e., the hood's ability to contain hazardous air contaminants) (National Research Council, 1995). The American Industrial Hygiene

Association recommends an average face velocity of 80 to 120 feet per minute for laboratory exhaust hoods (AIHA, 1992 in ANSI/AAMI, 1996).

Once glutaraldehyde vapor is collected inside a suitable exhaust hood, it is transported through a duct system and then discharged to the outside via a fan.

Ductless Fume Hoods

Ductless fume hoods are ventilated enclosures that have their own exhaust fan that draws air out of the hood, passes it through an air cleaning filter and then discharges the cleaned exhaust air back into the workplace. Ductless fume hoods are "recirculating" exhaust systems used for contaminant control and use a variety of filters for air cleaning purposes, depending on the air contaminant(s). For glutaraldehyde, a filter containing activated charcoal or other suitable sorbent material must be used to effectively capture vapors. Because the collection efficiency of these filters decreases over time, a preventive maintenance program in accordance with the manufacturer's recommendations must be implemented to ensure optimum performance of the system and effective employee protection.

Ductless fume hoods may also come equipped with a variety of features as specified in the American National Standards for Recirculation of Air from Industrial Process Exhaust Systems (ANSI/AIHA, 1998). These safety features are designed to prevent inadvertent exposure in the workplace and include continuous monitoring devices equipped with alarms to alert operators to potential filter break through, and backup air cleaning devices.

Transfer Procedures

Reducing the release of glutaraldehyde vapor during transfer operations can be accomplished by the use of automated and enclosed equipment. For example, the transfer of glutaraldehyde from drums into process containers can be automated using pumps and closed transfer lines. Such automated equipment can help employees avoid glutaraldehyde exposure (OSHA "Hospital

e-Tool;" http://www.osha.gov/SLTC/etools/hospital/index.html);
(AFSCME, 2001).

The use of a "safety nozzle" for pouring reduces the potential
for splashing and "glugging" during initial pouring of glutaraldehyde solutions. When using a "safety nozzle, " be aware that
droplets may remain inside the nozzle and take care to avoid
spraying droplets into the atmosphere when removing (unscrewing)
it from one container and screwing it onto another container.

Automated Disinfection

The use of automated processing equipment to disinfect
instruments can significantly reduce the glutaraldehyde exposures
of employees performing disinfection procedures, as well as of
other employees and non-employees in the vicinity. However,
exposure is still possible, especially when poor work practices are
used or the equipment is poorly designed or improperly installed.
The ANSI/ AAMI ST58 standard contains detailed guidelines (Figure
2, below) for the purchase and installation of automated equipment
which is now widely used in health care facilities that perform high-
volume disinfection.

**Figure 2.   Guidelines for the Purchase and Installation of
Automated Glutaraldehyde Processing Equipment**

Automated processing equipment encloses the glutaraldehyde
disinfection/sterilizing operations and can significantly reduce
the release of glutaraldehyde vapor into the workroom air
(compared with manual disinfection operations). However, the
equipment must be properly designed and installed in order to
control glutaraldehyde vapor effectively. The ANSI/AAMI ST58
standard contains detailed guidelines for the purchase and
installation of such equipment. Key points include the following:

1. Purchase automated processing equipment only from a manufacturer who can provide documentation (i.e., exposure
   monitoring data) of its effectiveness in controlling glutaraldehyde vapor releases.

(Figure 2. continued)

2. Other purchase considerations include: space needs, accessibility, safety features, mid-cycle inspection capability, and means of changing and disposing of glutaraldehyde solutions.

3. Following installation, the equipment performance should be evaluated before it is put into actual use at the facility. Exposure monitoring should be conducted to ensure that all equipment is performing properly.

Note: Properly installed ventilation is still necessary even with the use of automated glutaraldehyde processing equipment. For example, ventilation is needed to control exposure when glutaraldehyde is poured into the machine's reservoir and whenever the machine is opened to observe or troubleshoot the equipment. Ductless enclosure hoods are available in a variety of sizes, including custom designs, for automated processing equipment (freestanding and countertop units) from select medical/laboratory equipment suppliers.

Mobile Disinfecting Stations

Mobile disinfecting soaking stations designed specifically for manual high-level disinfecting provide an enclosed area for sterilizing trays, protecting employees from splashes and spills, and controlling exposure to vapor from glutaraldehyde and other disinfectants. Mobile disinfecting stations utilize ductless fume hoods for vapor control and may have different types of filters available depending on the disinfectant to be used.

Facility Design

The health care facility should designate central areas for disinfection and sterilization using glutaraldehyde so that specific controls can be utilized (ANSI/AAMI, 1996). Specific engineering controls are more difficult to implement in facilities that permit the widespread use of glutaraldehyde throughout the site. The centralized location should be large enough to permit freedom of movement (a crowded work space creates the potential for spills), and have limited access. Posting warning signs at the entrance to the centralized location and limiting access to only trained personnel designated to perform operations involving the use of glutaraldehyde will contribute to reducing exposure at the facility.

Recommended Work Practices

Poor work practices can contribute significantly to an employee's glutaraldehyde exposure. The health care facility should evaluate each glutaraldehyde-using operation and observe employees' work practices to determine all potential sources of exposure. Developing procedures for safe work practices may be useful for training and communication purposes. These procedures should emphasize prevention of employee contact with glutaraldehyde solution or vapors. Only trained, designated personnel should be responsible for handling glutaraldehyde. The following sections provide general recommendations for safe work practices addressing the transportation, storage, use, spill control, cleanup, and disposal of glutaraldehyde. Individual facilities should tailor their work practices to the specific glutaraldehyde operations in place at their work sites.

Transportation and Storage of Glutaraldehyde

- Transport glutaraldehyde solution only in closed containers with tight-fitting lids to minimize the potential for spills (NICNAS, 1994).
- Designate centralized locations for using glutaraldehyde to reduce the potential for spills during transport.
- Store unused glutaraldehyde solutions in tightly covered containers in a cool, secured, and properly labeled area (NICNAS, 1994; ANSI/AAMI, 1996).
- Dispose of outdated solutions properly.

Use and Handling Procedures

- When transferring glutaraldehyde to soaking basins and reservoirs, pour the liquid carefully and minimize splashing.

- Minimize splashing and agitation of glutaraldehyde solutions by careful placement and removal of instruments (NSW Health Department, 1993).
- When transferring and pouring glutaraldehyde solutions, use safety nozzles designed with a flexible spout and shut-off valve, when available (http://www.kemmed.com).
- Keep covers on soaking basins closed as much as possible and use appropriately-sized, tight-fitting lids for containers.
- Use appropriately-sized soaking basins designed to minimize surface area (e.g., narrow, deep container) (ANSI/AAMI, 1996).
- Keep automatic washer doors closed at all times except when necessary for loading or unloading of instruments to be disinfected.
- Rinse soaked instruments under gently running water as close as possible to the soaking tray or washer to contain solution and minimize dripping on other surfaces (NSW Health Department, 1993).
- Use adequate ventilation if using compressed air to dry instruments rinsed with ethyl or isopropyl alcohol rinses. See discussion on Engineering Controls at page 10 in this section.
- Use glutaraldehyde only in designated areas where traffic and ventilation can be controlled.
- Ensure that the ventilation system is operating prior to handling glutaraldehyde solutions. (Consult your facilities department for help on how to check the operation of your ventilation system.) NOTE: The odor threshold of glutaraldehyde has been reported to be 0.04 parts per million (ppm), and odor detection is a potential indicator that the engineering controls are inadequate. However, you cannot always rely on odor detection because some formulations may contain a perfume to mask the odor of glutaraldehyde (ANSI/AAMI, 1996). Additionally, individuals vary in their ability to detect odors; thus, the lack of an odor does not necessarily mean that exposures are adequately controlled.
- Follow recommended ACGIH procedures for proper use of laboratory hoods (see Figure 3 at page 19).

- Close workroom doors to ensure the effectiveness of any available general dilution ventilation (NJDOHSS, 1998).
- Do not store food, eat, drink, smoke, or apply cosmetics in any area where glutaraldehyde is stored or used.
- Clean up small glutaraldehyde spills and releases immediately. In the case of large spills or delayed response, employees should be encouraged to close doors, alert others and activate the HazMat spill response team.

Alternatives to Glutaraldehyde for High-Level Disinfection

When an alternative to glutaraldehyde is available which is at least as effective as an FDA-approved high-level disinfectant, consideration should be given to whether the alternative is safer for employees. Prior to selecting a specific glutaraldehyde alternative, in addition to process and product considerations, consideration should be given to the following: the toxicity of the glutaraldehyde alternative (e.g., there may be limited knowledge regarding the potential health effects of the alternative); disposal, ventilation, personal protective equipment (PPE) and air monitoring requirements.

Health care facilities that would like to eliminate or reduce their dependence on glutaraldehyde as a high-level disinfectant have two options: (1) use a different (drop-in) liquid chemical disinfectant (e.g., Cidex OPA, Compliance, Sporox II, and Sterilox); or (2) invest in new enclosed equipment technologies that do not utilize glutaraldehyde (e.g., Sterrad and Steris) (Sustainable Hospitals, 2001). Current alternatives to glutaraldehyde for high-level disinfection and/or sterilization can be found on the Food and Drug Administration's (FDA) website at www.fda.gov.cdrh/ode/germlab.html. Material Safety Data Sheets (MSDSs) for each product can be obtained directly from the manufacturer.

Selection and Use of Personal Protective Equipment

See the *General Recommendations* section of this publication at page 23 for additional information on the selection and use of personal protective equipment to control employee exposures to glutaraldehyde. General information on employee training, exposure monitoring, disposal of glutaraldehyde solutions, and spill and cleanup procedures applicable to the use of glutaraldehyde as a high-level disinfectant is also included.

GLUTARALDEHYDE USE AS A TISSUE FIXATIVE

Primary Sources of Glutaraldehyde Exposure

Glutaraldehyde is used in some health care facilities as a fixative in electron and light microscopy and as a tissue preservative. Laboratory personnel may be exposed to solutions containing up to 50% glutaraldehyde during the preparation of fixative solutions for use in microscopy and histology, and to very small quantities of working strength solutions (3-6%) during tissue fixation. If the use is regular and exposure controls are lacking or ineffective, adverse health effects may occur. Eye, skin, and respiratory irritation have been reported for laboratory personnel engaged in tissue fixing (NICNAS, 1994, NIOSH, 1986). The more serious effects, such as skin/respiratory tract sensitization and asthma, may occur in some exposed individuals.

NIOSH has measured and reported air concentrations of glutaraldehyde as high as 1.5 mg/m^3 (0.36 ppm) during tissue fixing operations evaluated during maintenance procedures (NIOSH, 1984). The following activities are the primary sources of glutaraldehyde exposure during its use as a tissue fixative:

- preparing glutaraldehyde solution from concentrate to fill enclosed fixing basin;
- draining and cleaning of fixing basin;
- removing and adding materials (e.g., tissue sample) to the fixing basin;
- handling materials fixed in the basin;

- handling tissue samples for refrigeration;
- rinsing tissue samples in a buffer;
- slicing tissue samples onto slides (NIOSH, 1986).

Recommended Exposure Controls

The use of a properly operating laboratory hood is the rec-ommended method of controlling the exposures of laboratory employees who use glutaraldehyde to prepare slides of tissue samples. As discussed above, for employees who perform instrument disinfection using glutaraldehyde, respirators should not be the primary means of controlling exposure during these laboratory operations. Appropriate PPE, such as gloves and safety eyewear, should always be used <u>in combination</u> with the laboratory hood. Guidelines for the proper use of laboratory hoods are presented in Figure 3, below. These guidelines were developed by the American Conference of Governmental Industrial Hygienists (ACGIH).

Figure 3.   Recommended Work Practices for Laboratory Hoods

1. Keep all equipment at least 6 inches inside the hood.
2. Keep your head outside of the hood during all operations involving hazardous chemicals.
3. Do not store chemicals or laboratory equipment inside the hood.
4. Keep the hood sash closed as much as possible.
5. Do not allow equipment to obstruct the air exhaust slots inside the hood.
6. Avoid turbulence at the hood face by minimizing activity in the vicinity of the hood.
7. Keep doors and windows closed when the hood is operating (exception: where laboratories are designed to keep doors open).
8. Keep the hood sash at the proper operating height. Site Safety and Health or Facilities personnel can provide assistance in evaluating the hood to determine the hood sash location that ensures optimum operation.

Source: ACGIH *Industrial Ventilation*, 2001.

Selection and Use of Personal Protective Equipment

See the *General Recommendations* section of this publication at page 23 for additional information on the selection and use of personal protective equipment to control exposures to glutaraldehyde. General information on employee training, exposure monitoring, disposal of glutaraldehyde solutions and spill and cleanup procedures applicable to the use of glutaraldehyde as a tissue fixative is also included.

GLUTARALDEHYDE USE IN X-RAY PROCESSING

Primary Sources of Glutaraldehyde Exposure

Health care facilities employees who develop x-rays may be exposed to glutaraldehyde during such operations. Glutaraldehyde is used in developing solutions as a hardening agent to shorten the drying cycle in film processing. X-ray developers are typically supplied as a concentrate containing 30-50% weight-to-weight ratio glutaraldehyde and are diluted to working strength solutions containing less than 1-2% glutaraldehyde. Automatic mixers are generally used to mix and dispense developing solutions; however, smaller radiology units may still use manual methods. The primary sources of glutaraldehyde exposure during x-ray processing are as follows:

- mixing glutaraldehyde developer solutions;
- adding solutions to tanks and processors;
- processing x-rays;
- removing incompletely dried processed x-rays;
- cleaning rollers and tanks on x-ray machines;
- emptying tanks and processors;
- fugitive emissions from open tanks and leaky hoses and equipment; and
- automatic processor exhaust.

(Source: NICNAS, 1994.)

Measurements of health care employee exposure to glutaraldehyde during x-ray film processing generally show glutaraldehyde levels below recommended exposure standards, especially with automatic mixing and processing operations. Efforts to minimize or eliminate occupational exposure are recommended because glutaraldehyde is a potential sensitizer, health effects may occur at levels lower than current standards, and the effects of simultaneous exposure to multiple chemicals used in developer and fixer solutions are not clearly understood (NICNAS, 1994; Teschke et al., 2002).

Recommended Exposure Controls

As described for previous operations, the primary method of exposure control is enclosing the operation and installing local exhaust ventilation. The following sections describe methods of exposure control during x-ray processing.

Alternative Processes

A good method of glutaraldehyde exposure control is substitution with a safer process that does not require the use of glutaraldehyde. There are commercially available processes that do not require glutaraldehyde as a hardener (Thunthy et al., 1994). Digital x-ray processors are also a viable substitute.

Engineering Controls

Where alternative processes cannot be implemented, engineering controls should be implemented to minimize glutaraldehyde exposure during film processing operations. Examples of engineering controls include:

- installing automatic mixers and processors equipped with local exhaust ventilation that is discharged to outdoors;
- conducting manual mixing and processing within laboratory fume hoods;
- using sealed containers and dispensing units for automatic transfer of glutaraldehyde solutions to processors;
- maintaining glutaraldehyde work areas under slight negative

pressure to prevent glutaraldehyde emissions from escaping into surrounding areas;

- keeping darkroom and processing temperatures as low as possible to minimize glutaraldehyde evaporation.

(Source: NICNAS, 1994.)

Recommended Work Practices

Safe work practices for the use and handling of glutaraldehyde in x-ray film processing include the following:

- regular inspection and maintenance of auto mixers and processors to prevent vapor releases due to leaks and overheating;
- placement and use of mixing tanks and glutaraldehyde solutions in laboratory fume hoods or other enclosed, well ventilated areas;
- careful mixing and handling procedures to minimize vapor release, splashing, spillage, and skin contact;
- use of tight-fitting lids on mixing tanks;
- use of adequately-sized and properly located washing receptacles for cleaning processor equipment and tanks;
- limited handling of wet films; and
- immediate cleanup of small glutaraldehyde spills and releases. See the paragraph on large spills in the *General Recommendations* section of this document at page 31.

(Source: NICNAS, 1994.)

Selection and Use of Personal Protective Equipment

See the *General Recommendations* section of this publication, below, for additional information on the selection and use of personal protective equipment. General information on employee training, exposure monitoring, disposal of glutaraldehyde solutions and spill and cleanup procedures applicable to the use of glutaraldehyde in x-ray processing is also included.

The following recommendations apply to all health care operations involving glutaraldehyde use, and cover:

- selection and use of personal protective equipment;
- employee information and training;
- exposure monitoring;
- disposal of glutaraldehyde solutions; and
- spill control and cleanup procedures.

Selection and Use of Personal Protective Equipment

Employees must wear personal protective equipment (PPE) designed to protect skin and eyes from contact with glutaraldehyde solutions (29 CFR 1910.132 and 1910.133). Contact with clothing should also be prevented. The health care facility should develop and implement a written program outlining the facility's policies and procedures for PPE selection and use, including a hazard assessment and written certification that the hazard assessment has been performed (pursuant to the requirements of 29 CFR 1910.132) to determine the nature of the hazards requiring PPE.

Skin Protection

Employers must select and require employees to use appropriate hand protection when employees' hands are exposed to potential skin absorption of substances such as glutaraldehyde (29 CFR 1910.138). Gloves impervious to glutaraldehyde are required to be worn to prevent contact with glutaraldehyde solutions. Elbow-length gloves or protective sleeves made of glutaraldehyde-impervious material should be worn to protect the hands and forearms (ANSI/AAMI, 1996). The gloves used will depend on the type of work to be done, the duration of contact, and the concentration of glutaraldehyde. Among the chemical-protective materials, *butyl rubber, nitrile* and *Viton®* are the most impervious to 50% glutaraldehyde solutions and have been shown to provide full shift protection against glutaraldehyde permeation (Jordan et al.,

1996; Forsberg and Keith, 1999). For shorter exposures, gloves made of polyethylene and styrene-butadiene/styrene-isoprene copolymers (i.e., Allergard Synthetic Surgical Gloves) provide protection for several hours with dilute (2% to 3.4%) glutaraldehyde solutions (Jordan et al., 1996; Ansell Health Care, 2003).

Latex examination gloves may not provide adequate skin protection against glutaraldehyde. Although one author reports a breakthrough time of 45 minutes with latex examination gloves and standard 2% to 3.4% glutaraldehyde solutions, other materials are available that provide a greater margin of safety. Therefore, latex gloves are not recommended for use with glutaraldehyde.

Polyvinyl chloride (PVC) and neoprene gloves do not provide adequate protection and should not be used with glutaraldehyde solutions because they may retain or absorb glutaraldehyde (Jordan et al., 1996).

If the required hazard assessment (29 CFR 1910.132) indicates a need for additional protection for skin and clothing, it can be provided through the use of isolation gowns, lab coats, or aprons (plus sleeve protectors) that are made of glutaraldehyde-impervious material such as polyethylene-coated, spun-bond polypropylene. Protective clothing that has become saturated should be removed quickly and laundered prior to reuse. If skin contact with glutaraldehyde occurs, the skin should be washed thoroughly with soap and water for at least 15 minutes (ANSI/AAMI, 1996).

Eye Protection
Splashproof goggles or safety glasses with full face shields must be worn wherever there is potential for glutaraldehyde solution to contact the eyes (29 CFR 1910.133). Suitable emergency eyewash equipment must be immediately available for quick drenching or flushing of the eyes (for at least 15 minutes) in all glutaraldehyde usage locations. It is recommended that emergency eyewash units be accessible and located within a 10 second travel time of all affected areas. For additional details, consult American National Standard Z358.1-1998, Emergency Eyewash and Shower Equipment.

If an eyewash and a shower are required, a combination unit should be considered.

Respiratory Protection

Respirators should not be used as a substitute for installing effective engineering controls. When effective engineering controls are not feasible, or while they are being implemented, appropriate respirators may be used to control employee exposure to glutaraldehyde vapor (29 CFR 1910.134(a)(1)).

All personnel who may be required to wear a respirator for routine or emergency use must be included in a written respiratory protection program that meets the requirements of OSHA's Respiratory Protection standard (29 CFR 1910.134). Such a program must have written site-specific procedures for selecting, using, and maintaining respirators; medical evaluations; fit testing; employee training; and routine program evaluation.

Employers must select appropriate respirators based on an exposure assessment or a reasonable estimate of employee exposures to glutaraldehyde vapor during routine and/or emergency work procedures. For protection against exposures to glutaraldehyde vapor during routine procedures, employers may provide air-purifying respirators (i.e., a half-face or full-face air-purifying respirator with organic vapor cartridges), or air-supplying respirators.

If air-purifying respirators are provided, employers must implement a change-out schedule for air-purifying canisters and cartridges to ensure that they are changed before the end of their service life. Change-out schedules must be developed by consulting the respirator manufacturer cartridge or canister test data and evaluating workplace conditions such as estimated glutaraldehyde concentrations, temperature, relative humidity, and employee breathing rate. Cartridge or canister service life calculation formulas are also available on the OSHA website, www.osha.gov.

Air-supplied respirators should be used when exposures may be reasonably anticipated to be higher and for unknown exposures, such as emergency spill situations.

All respirators used must be certified by the National Institute for Occupational Safety and Health (NIOSH) and must be appropriate for use with glutaraldehyde (29 CFR 1910.134(d)(1)(i) and (ii)). The disposable air-purifying particulate respirators (filtering facepieces) are not effective against organic vapors, and must not be used for glutaraldehyde protection.

Employees who voluntarily choose to wear respirators, but who are not required by their employers or OSHA to wear a respirator, must still receive the information in Appendix D to 29 CFR 1910.134. See OSHA's Respiratory Protection standard, 29 CFR 1910.134, for further details regarding the requirements for employee use of respirators.

Employee Information and Training

All employers with glutaraldehyde solutions or other hazardous chemicals in their workplaces must develop and implement a written hazard communication program that meets the requirements of OSHA's Hazard Communication standard, 29 CFR 1910.1200. Such a program must include provisions for employee access to material safety data sheets (MSDSs), container labeling, and training for all potentially exposed individuals.

Employees who use, handle, or may have potential exposure (e.g., accidental or possible) to glutaraldehyde solutions must be provided information and training prior to their initial work assignment. Employees must be provided information regarding the requirements of the Hazard Communication standard; operations in their work area where glutaraldehyde solutions (and other hazardous chemicals) are present; and the location and availability of the written hazard communication program and material safety data sheets (MSDSs).

Employee training must include, at a minimum, the following elements (29 CFR 1910.1200):

- methods and observations that may be used to detect the presence or release of glutaraldehyde in the workplace;
- the physical and health hazards of glutaraldehyde;
- the measures employees can take to protect themselves, including specific procedures the employer has implemented to protect employees from exposure to glutaraldehyde, such as appropriate work practices, emergency procedures, and personal protective equipment; and

- an explanation of the material safety data sheet, the employer's labeling system, and how employees can obtain and use the appropriate hazard information.

Exposure Monitoring

Workplace exposure monitoring should be conducted to ensure a safe work environment and to compare monitoring results with recommended occupational exposure limits for glutaraldehyde. Monitoring should be conducted after initiating use of glutaraldehyde solutions; whenever there is a significant change in protocol, work practices, caseload, or workplace ventilation systems; and after major equipment (e.g., endoscope washers or other automated equipment) repairs (ANSI/AAMI, 1996). Exposure monitoring should also be conducted if employees have complaints or symptoms of glutaraldehyde exposure.

Monitoring should be conducted in all glutaraldehyde use areas as well as in the breathing zone of each employee using or handling glutaraldehyde solutions. Special attention should be given to short-term tasks that may have elevated exposures such as pouring, mixing or otherwise agitating glutaraldehyde solutions.

Several air sampling methods are available for monitoring glutaraldehyde exposures. These methods include active and passive sampling techniques as well as the use of a direct-reading instrument. Active air sampling uses battery-powered personal sampling pumps and treated filters or sorbent tubes for sample collection. Passive sampling uses small, lightweight, easy-to-use badge assemblies that rely on natural air movement rather than pumps for sample collection. After sampling, the filters or sorbent tubes and passive monitors should be sent to a laboratory for analysis. Accredited laboratories have demonstrated their ability to meet performance standards and are preferred. The OSHA website at www.osha.gov/dts/sltc/methods/organic/org064/org064.html and NIOSH at www.cdc.gov/niosh/nmam/pdfs/2532.pdf may be consulted for additional information regarding validated sampling and analytical methods for glutaraldehyde. In addition, the American Industrial Hygiene Association (www.aiha.org) may be consulted for a listing of consultants and accredited industrial hygiene laboratories.

A direct-reading, handheld, easy-to-use, portable instrument called the "Glutaraldemeter" may also be used to compare monitoring results with recommended glutaraldehyde exposure limits as well as to determine concentrations resulting from spills and other emergencies.

Active air sampling methods require sampling expertise and special sampling supplies and should be performed by an industrial hygienist or other qualified professional trained in industrial hygiene air sampling strategies and techniques. Passive monitors and the Glutaraldemeter do not necessarily require sampling expertise and can be used by health care personnel to evaluate workplace exposures. Proper use of passive monitors may be determined by consulting the manufacturer's instructions and/or the laboratory that will conduct the analyses. Proper use and maintenance of the Glutaraldemeter may be determined by consulting the equipment manufacturer (e.g., MSA or PPM Technology).

Active sampling methods are more sensitive and reliable than passive monitors/badges and the Glutaraldemeter. Quantitative limits of detection (LOD) for the active methods are in the range of 0.44 ppb (parts per billion), while the reliable LOD for passive methods and the Glutaraldemeter are in the range of 20-100 ppb.

Disposal of Glutaraldehyde Solutions

Dispose of glutaraldehyde solutions in accordance with local, state, and Federal regulations. Check with your local Publicly Owned Treatment Works (POTW) to determine if glutaraldehyde solutions can be disposed of in the sanitary sewer system. Some POTWs may prohibit the disposal of glutaraldehyde solutions in the sanitary sewer system or may require neutralization prior to disposal. If there are no disposal restrictions, glutaraldehyde solutions may be disposed of, along with copious amounts of cold water, into a drain connected to the sanitary sewer system. Do not discard glutaraldehyde solutions (including neutralized solutions) into septic systems. Unlike municipal sewage treatment systems, septic systems are not diluted by other waste streams. Consequently, glutaraldehyde concentrations entering the system may be higher and have an adverse effect on the microorganisms that are necessary for proper functioning of the septic system. Dispose of empty glutaraldehyde containers according to product label instructions.

Spill Control and Cleanup Procedures

All glutaraldehyde spills have the potential to create vapor concentrations that exceed recommended exposure limits. Vayas et al. (2000) measured airborne concentrations during two spills that occurred during their study. The TWA exposures to glutaraldehyde were 0.27 mg/m^3 (0.06 ppm) for a spill of about one liter in an unventilated room, and 0.439 mg/m^3 (0.11 ppm) for a spill greater than 5 liters in a positive pressure theater. Niven et al. (1997) also reported on glutaraldehye monitoring results (as high as 1.4 ppm) from various spill scenarios. Consequently, a suitable plan of action with procedures for handling glutaraldehyde spills should be developed and implemented by knowledgeable and responsible individuals at the facility. In the development of this plan, consideration should be given to the physical characteristics of the area(s) where glutaraldehyde solutions are used (e.g., type and effectiveness of ventilation, room size and temperature) as well as the quantity and concentration(s) of the solution(s). The spill control plan should incorporate the following key elements (ANSI/AAMI, 1996):

- designation of individuals responsible for managing spill cleanup;
- evacuation procedures for nonessential personnel, if necessary;
- medical treatment procedures for exposed individuals;
- site-specific reporting requirements (e.g., site safety and health personnel);
- cleanup procedures, the location of spill control supplies, and required personal protective equipment;
- location and availability of material safety data sheets (MSDSs) for glutaraldehyde-based sterilants/disinfectants and manufacturer recommendations for emergency response;

- employee training requirements;
- air exchange rate(s) within the areas of use and procedures to prevent the dispersal of glutaraldehyde vapor to other areas of the facility through the general ventilation system; and
- respiratory protection program requirements pertaining to glutaraldehyde.

General Procedures

All spills should be cleaned up immediately, regardless of size. All necessary spill cleanup equipment (e.g., sponges, towels, absorbent mats/wipes, spill pillows, mop and bucket, plastic dust-pan and trash bags) and personal protective equipment (i.e., eye, hand, body and respiratory protection) should be readily available. Whether or not a spill can be cleaned up safely without the use of neutralizing chemicals and/or a respirator will depend on a number of factors such as the glutaraldehyde concentration and the amount spilled, the temperature of the room and the solution, and the effectiveness of the ventilation in the spill area. (ANSI/AAMI, 1996). Any spill larger than a drip or a splash may need to be neutralized; and, when vapor concentrations are unknown, air-supplied or atmosphere-supplying respirators are appropriate.

Neutralizing Chemicals

Before using any type of glutaraldehyde-based product, review the manufacturer's recommendations for spill cleanup. Several chemicals can be used to lower the glutaraldehyde concentration in solutions and/or the ambient vapor level during a spill. Examples include household ammonia, ammonium carbonate powder, dibasic ammonium phosphate, and sodium bisulfite. Glycine is also used as a neutralizer, and may be less hazardous than others. There are also commercially available products for this purpose (ANSI/AAMI, 1996), including powders, solutions, and salts.

Drips and Splashes

A reusable or disposable sponge, towel, or mop may be used to quickly clean up small spills. Glutaraldehyde solutions can also be neutralized with an appropriate chemical agent before wiping up with a sponge, towel, or mop. Cleanup supplies should be thoroughly rinsed with large amounts of water prior to reuse. Rinse water and disposable cleanup supplies should be discarded according to applicable regulations as well as the procedures outlined in the facility spill control plan (ANSI/AAMI, 1996).

Drips and splashes may also be cleaned up with commercially available spill control kits that contain mats/wipes to absorb and neutralize small spills. The absorbed medium should be disposed of according to local, state and Federal regulations.

Large Spills

Any glutaraldehyde spill larger than small drips or splashes should be cleaned up by properly trained and equipped spill response personnel. Certain larger spills of glutaraldehyde are covered by the requirements of OSHA's Hazardous Waste Operations and Emergency Response standard (29 CFR 1910.120(q)).

Pre-planning for spills is a critical piece of the facility exposure control plan. Personnel should understand the necessity to evacuate until the spill is cleaned up and the worksite is safe for reentry of employees. Appropriate spill-response equipment placed outside the affected area for access after the area is evacuated will facilitate compliance with the emergency spill response plan. Supplied air respirators are an important component of a spill-response kit. Appropriate training on the use of the respirators is an important piece of the pre-spill planning, so that spill responders are adequately equipped and trained.

Large spills should be contained and neutralized or contained and collected for disposal. Once contained, spills may be neutralized with an appropriate chemical agent such as sodium bisulfite (2-3 parts (by weight) per part of glutaraldehyde solution) with a contact time of 5 minutes at room temperature, using a mop or other tool to thoroughly blend in the deactivation compound. A less hazardous neutralizer, glycine, can be used in a ratio of 25 grams per gallon of 2.4% glutaraldehyde solution to neutralize in 5 minutes. Depending on the size of the spill and site conditions, heat and vapor may be liberated by the reaction with the neutralizing chemicals (ANSI/AAMI, 1996). Commercially available spill pillows and booms may also be used to easily contain, absorb, and/or neutralize large glutaraldehyde spills.

After the glutaraldehyde solution is removed, the spill area and the cleanup supplies/tools should be thoroughly rinsed with large amounts of cold water. Rinse water, disposable cleanup supplies and absorbent medium (if used) should be disposed of according to applicable regulations and the procedures outlined in the facility spill control plan (ANSI/AAMI, 1996).

Additional Resources

Rutala, W.A. 1996. APIC Guideline for Selection and Use of Disinfectants. *Am J Infect Control*, 24:313-42.

Environmental Protection Agency (EPA). 2002. Replacing ethylene oxide and glutaraldehyde. Online at http://www.ciwmb. ca.gov/wpie/healthcare/EPAEtOGlut.pdf

National Institute for Occupational Safety and Health (NIOSH). 2001. Glutaraldehyde: occupational hazards in hospitals. Online at http://cdc.gov/niosh/2001-115html

References

ACGIH, 2001. Industrial Ventilation – A Manual of Recommended Practice. American Conference of Governmental Industrial Hygienists. 24th Edition. Cincinnati, OH. ACGIH.

ACGIH, 2004. Documentation of the Threshold Limit Values and Biological Exposure Indices. American Conference of Governmental Industrial Hygienists. 7th Edition. 2004 Supplement, ACGIH.

AFSCME Health and Safety Program 2001. Fact Sheet, Glutaraldehyde. 1625 L Street, N.W., Washington, DC 20036, and online.

Ansell Health Care. 2003. Allergard® II Sterile Synthetic Copolymer Surgical Gloves. [Technical Data Sheet]. Red Bank, NJ: Ansell Health Care.

ANSI/AAMI. 1996. ST58. American National Standard for the Safe use and handling of glutaraldehyde-based products in health care facilities. Arlington, VA: Association for the Advancement of Medical Instrumentation.

ANSI/AIHA (Z9.7) 1998. American National Standard for Recirculation of Air from Industrial Process Exhaust Systems. Fairfax, VA: American Industrial Hygiene Association.

APIC Guideline. 1994. APIC Guideline for Infection Prevention and Control in Flexible Endoscopy. Association for Professionals in Infection Control and Epidemiology. APIC, Inc. 1994.

Ballantyne, B. and B. Berman. 1984. Dermal sensitizing potential of glutaraldehyde: a review and recent observations. *J Toxicol Cutaneous Ocul Toxicol* 3(3):251-262.

Butt, G., Greenley, P., Herrick, R., and L. DiBerardinis. 1999. Exposure to glutaraldehyde vapors during endoscopic sterilization processes in a large research and teaching institution. *Journal of Healthcare Safety, Compliance & Infection Control* 3(4): 172179.

Crandall, M.S. 1987. Montgomery Hospital, Norristown, PA., NIOSH Health Hazard Evaluation Report No. 86-226-1769. NIOSH.

Di Stefano, F., Siriruttanapruk, S., McCoach, J. and P. Sherwood Burge. 1999. Glutaraldehyde: an occupational hazard in the hospital setting. *Allergy* 54:1105-1109.

Ellet, M.L., Mikels, C.A., and J.W. Fullhart. 1995. SGNA Endoscopic Disinfectant Survey. *Gastroenterol Nurs* 18(1):2-10.

FDA. 2003. FDA-Cleared Sterilants and High Level Disinfectants with General Claims for Processing Reusable Medical and Dental Devices. U.S. Department of Health and Human Services, Food and Drug Administration, Center for Devices and Radiological Health. Online at http://www.fda.gov/cdrh/ode/germlab.html

Forsberg, K., and L.H. Keith. 1997. Chemical Protective Clothing Performance Index. 2nd Edition. New York: John Wiley & Sons, Inc., pp. 326-327.

Fowler J.F., Jr. 1989. Allergic contact dermatitis from glutaraldehyde exposure. *J Occup Environ Med*, 31(10):852-853.

Gannon, P.F.G., Bright, P., Campbell, M., O'Hickey, S.P., and P.S. Burge. 1995. Occupational asthma due to glutaraldehyde and formaldehyde in endoscopy and x-ray departments. *Thorax*, 50:156-159.

Health & Safety Executive, UK. 1997. Glutaraldehyde criteria document for an occupational exposure, ISBN 07176 1443 3.

Jordan, S.L.P., Stowers, M.F., Trawick, E.G., and A.B. Theis. 1996. Glutaraldehyde permeation: choosing the proper glove. *Am J Infect Control*, 24(2):67-69.

Keynes, H.L., Ross, D.J. and J.C. McDonald. 1996. SWORD '95: Surveillance of work-related and occupational respiratory disease in the U.K. *Occup Med* 46(5):379-381.

Maibach, H.I. and S.D. Prystowsky. 1977. Glutaraldehyde (pentanedial) allergic contact dermatitis. *Arch Dermatol* 113:170-171.

Marzulli, F.N. and H.I. Maibach. 1974. The use of graded con-centrations in studying skin sensitizers: experimental contact sensitization in man. *Food Cosmet Toxicol*, 12: 219-227.

Naidu, V., S. Lam, and G. O'Donnell. 1995. Typical glu-taraldehyde vapour levels in endoscope disinfection units in New South Wales hospitals. *J Occup Health and Safety* - Austral NZ 11(1): 43-57.

National Research Council. 1995. Prudent Practices in the Laboratory – Handling and Disposal of Chemicals. Washington, D.C.: National Academy Press.

Nethercott, J.R., and D.L. Holness. 1988. Contact dermatitis in funeral service workers. *Contact Dermatitis*, 18:263-267.

Nethercott J.R., Holness D.L., and E. Page. 1988. Occupational contact dermatitis due to glutaraldehyde in health care workers. *Contact Dermatitis*, 18:193-196.

NICNAS, 1994. Priority Existing Chemical No. 3, Glutaraldehyde, Full Public Report, http://www.nicnas.gov.au/publications/CAR/PEC/PEC3/PEC3index.htm

National Industrial Chemicals Notification and Assessment Scheme, Australian Government Publishing Service, Canberra.

NIOSH. 1984. Health Hazard Evaluation Report No. HETA 83-074-1525. National Jewish Hospital, Denver, Colorado. U.S. Department of Health and Human Services, Public Health Service, Centers for Disease Control, National Institute for Occupational Safety and Health, Cincinnati, OH.

NIOSH. 1986. Health Hazard Evaluation Report No. HETA 84-535-1690. National Jewish Hospital, Denver, Colorado. U.S. Department of Health and Human Services, Public Health Service, Centers for Disease Control, National Institute for Occupational Safety and Health, Cincinnati, OH.

NIOSH. 1987. Health Hazard Evaluation Report No. HETA-85-257-1791. Mercy Medical Center, Denver, Colorado. U.S. Department of Health and Human Services, Public Health Service, Centers for Disease Control, National Institute for Occupational Safety and Health, Cincinnati, OH.

NIOSH. 1991. Health Hazard Evaluation Report No. HETA-90-296-2149. Monongalia General Hospital, Morgantown, West Virginia. U.S. Department of Health and Human Services, Public Health Service, Centers for Disease Control, National Institute for Occupational Safety and Health, Cincinnati, OH.

NIOSH. 2001. Glutaraldehyde: Occupational Hazards in Hospitals. DHHS (NIOSH) Publication No. 2001-115. U.S. Department of Health and Human Services, Centers for Disease Control and Prevention, National Institute for Occupational Safety and Health, Cincinnati, OH.

Niven, K.J.M., Cherrie, J.W. and J. Spencer. 1997. Estimation of exposure from spilled glutaraldehyde solutions in a hospital setting. *Ann Occup Hyg*, 41(6):691-698.

NJDOHSS. 1998. Glutaraldehyde survey. New Jersey Department of Health and Senior Services, Occupational Disease and Injury Services, Trenton, NJ.

Norbäck, D. 1988. Skin and respiratory symptoms from exposure to alkaline glutaraldehyde in medical services. *Scand J Work Environ Health*, 14:366-371.

Nova Scotia Department of Environment and Labour, 2000. Glutaraldehyde Hazard Alert. Occupational Health and Safety Division. Hazard Alerts.

NSW Health Department. 1993. Guidelines for the Safe Use of Glutaraldehyde in Health Care Establishments - Amendment (http://www.health.nsw.gov.au/fcsd/rmc/cib/circulars/1993/cir93-99.pdf), North Sydney, Australia, File No. 1225/3, Circular No. 93/99.

Occupational Safety and Health Administration, online at: http://www.osha.gov

Pryor, P.D., 1984. National Jewish Hospital, Denver, Colorado. NIOSH Health Hazard Evaluation Report No. 83-074-1525.

Pisaniello, D.L., Gun, R.T., Tkaczuk, M.N., Nitshcke, M. and J. Crea. 1997. Glutaraldehyde exposures and symptoms among endoscopy nurses in South Australia. *Appl Occup Environ Hyg*, 12(3):171-177.

Rosenman, K.D., Reilly, M.J. and D.J. Kalinowski. 1997. A state-based surveillance system for work-related asthma. *J Occup Environ Med*, 39(5):415-425.

Sustainable Hospitals. 2001. The Lowell Center for Sustainable Production. Sustainable Hospitals Project. Glutaraldehyde control in hospitals. Available online at http://www.sustainablehospitals.org/HTMLSrc/IP_Glutcontrol.html

Stern, M.L., et al. Contact hypersensitivity response to glutaraldehyde in guinea pigs and mice. *Toxicol Ind Health*, 5(1):31-43, 1989.

Teschke, K., Chow, Y., Brauer, M., Chessor, E., Hirtle, B., Kennedy, S.M., Yeung, M.C. and H.D. Ward. 2002. Exposures and their determinants in radiographic film processing. *Am Ind Hyg Assoc J*, 63:11-21.

Thunthy, K.H., Yeadon, W.R. and R.Winberg. 1994. Sensitometric and archival evaluation of Kodak RA films in dental automatic processing. *Oral Surg Oral Med Oral Pathol*, 77(4):427-430.

University of North Carolina-Chapel Hill Health and Safety Manual. http://www.ehs.unc.edu/manuals/HSMManual/Chapter5html/h5-03.htm

Vyas, A., Pickering, C.A., Oldham, L.A., Francis, H.C., Fletcher, A.M., Merrett, T., and R. M. Niven. 2000. Survey of symptoms, respiratory function, and immunology and their relation to glutaraldehyde and other occupational exposures among endoscopy nursing staff. *Occup Environ Med*, 57:752-759.

Waters, A., Beach, J., and M. Abramson. 2003. Symptoms and lung function in health care personnel exposed to glutaraldehyde. *Am J Ind Med*, 43:196-203.

OSHA can provide extensive help through a variety of programs, including technical assistance about effective safety and health programs, state plans, workplace consultations, voluntary pro-tection programs, strategic partnerships, training and education, and more. An overall commitment to workplace safety and health can add value to your business, to your workplace and to your life.

Safety and Health Program Management Guidelines

Effective management of employee safety and health protection is a decisive factor in reducing the extent and severity of work-related injuries and illnesses and their related costs. In fact, an effective safety and health program forms the basis of good employee protection and can save time and money (about $4 for every dollar spent) and increase productivity and reduce employee injuries, illnesses and related workers' compensation costs.

To assist employers and employees in developing effective safety and health programs, OSHA published recommended *Safety and Health Program Management Guidelines* (54 *Federal Register* (16): 3904-3916, January 26, 1989). These voluntary guidelines apply to all places of employment covered by OSHA.

The guidelines identify four general elements critical to the development of a successful safety and health management program:

- Management leadership and employee involvement.
- Work analysis.
- Hazard prevention and control.
- Safety and health training.

The guidelines recommend specific actions, under each of these general elements, to achieve an effective safety and health program. The *Federal Register* notice is available online at www.osha.gov

State Programs

The Occupational Safety and Health Act of 1970 (OSH Act) en-courages states to develop and operate their own job safety and health plans. OSHA approves and monitors these plans. Twenty-four states, Puerto Rico and the Virgin Islands currently operate approved state plans: 22 cover both private and public (state and local government) employment; Connecticut, New Jersey, New York and the Virgin Islands cover the public sector only. States and territories with their own OSHA-approved occupational safety and health plans must adopt standards identical to, or at least as effective as, the Federal standards.

Consultation Services

Consultation assistance is available on request to employers who want help in establishing and maintaining a safe and healthful workplace. Largely funded by OSHA, the service is provided at no cost to the employer. Primarily developed for smaller employers with more hazardous operations, the consultation service is de-livered by state governments employing professional safety and health consultants. Comprehensive assistance includes an appraisal of all mechanical systems, work practices and occupational safety and health hazards of the workplace and all aspects of the em-ployer's present job safety and health program. In addition, the service offers assistance to employers in developing and imple-menting an effective safety and health program. No penalties are proposed or citations issued for hazards identified by the con-sultant. OSHA provides consultation assistance to the employer with the assurance that his or her name and firm and any infor-mation about the workplace will not be routinely reported to OSHA enforcement staff.

Under the consultation program, certain exemplary employers may request participation in OSHA's Safety and Health Achievement Recognition Program (SHARP). Eligibility for participa-tion in SHARP includes receiving a comprehensive consultation visit, demonstrating exemplary achievements in workplace safety and health by abating all identified hazards and developing an excellent safety and health program.

Employers accepted into SHARP may receive an exemption from programmed inspections (not complaint or accident investiga-tion inspections) for a period of one year. For more information concerning consultation assistance, see the OSHA website at www.osha.gov

Voluntary Protection Programs (VPP)

Voluntary Protection Programs and on-site consultation services, when coupled with an effective enforcement program, expand employee protection to help meet the goals of the *OSH Act*. The three levels of VPP are Star, Merit, and Star Demonstration designed to recognize outstanding achievements by companies that have successfully incorporated comprehensive safety and health programs into their total management system. The VPPs motivate others to achieve excellent safety and health results in the same outstanding way as they establish a cooperative relationship between employers, employees and OSHA.

For additional information on VPP and how to apply, contact the OSHA regional offices listed at the end of this publication.

Strategic Partnership Program

OSHA's Strategic Partnership Program, the newest member of OSHA's cooperative programs, helps encourage, assist and recognize the efforts of partners to eliminate serious workplace hazards and achieve a high level of employee safety and health. Whereas OSHA's Consultation Program and VPP entail one-on-one relationships between OSHA and individual worksites, most strategic partnerships seek to have a broader impact by building cooperative relationships with groups of employers and employees. These partnerships are voluntary, cooperative relationships between OSHA, employers, employee representatives and others (e.g., labor unions, trade and professional associations, universities and other government agencies).

For more information on this and other cooperative programs, contact your nearest OSHA office, or visit OSHA's website at www.osha.gov

Alliance Programs

The Alliance Program enables organizations committed to workplace safety and health to collaborate with OSHA to prevent injuries and illnesses in the workplace. OSHA and the Alliance participants work together to reach out to, educate and lead the nation's employers and their employees in improving and advancing workplace safety and health.

Groups that can form an Alliance with OSHA include employers, labor unions, trade or professional groups, educational institutions and government agencies. In some cases, organizations may be building on existing relationships with OSHA that were developed through other cooperative programs.

There are few formal program requirements for Alliances and the agreements do not include an enforcement component. However, OSHA and the participating organizations must define, implement and meet a set of short- and long-term goals that fall into three categories: training and education; outreach and communication; and promoting the national dialogue on workplace safety and health.

OSHA Training and Education

OSHA area offices offer a variety of information services, such as compliance assistance, technical advice, publications, audio-visual aids and speakers for special engagements. OSHA's Training Institute in Arlington Heights, IL, provides basic and advanced courses in safety and health for Federal and state compliance officers, state consultants, Federal agency personnel, and private sector employers, employees and their representatives.

The OSHA Training Institute also has established OSHA Training Institute Education Centers to address the increased demand for its courses from the private sector and from other Federal agencies. These centers are nonprofit colleges, universities and other organizations that have been selected after a competition for participation in the program.

OSHA also provides funds to nonprofit organizations, through grants, to conduct workplace training and education in subjects where OSHA believes there is a lack of workplace training. Grants are awarded annually. Grant recipients are expected to contribute 20 percent of the total grant cost.

For more information on grants, training and education, contact the OSHA Training Institute, Office of Training and Education, 2020 South Arlington Heights Road, Arlington Heights, IL 60005, (847) 297-4810 or see "Training" on OSHA's website at www.osha.gov. For further information on any OSHA program, contact your nearest OSHA area or regional office listed at the end of this publication.

Information Available Electronically

OSHA has a variety of materials and tools available on its website at www.osha.gov. These include *e-Tools* such as *Expert Advisors, Electronic Compliance Assistance Tools (e-cats), Technical Links*; regulations, directives and publications; videos and other information for employers and employees. OSHA's software programs and compliance assistance tools walk you through challenging safety and health issues and common problems to find the best solutions for your workplace.

A wide variety of OSHA materials, including standards, interpretations, directives, and more, can be purchased on CD-ROM from the U.S. Government Printing Office, Superintendent of Documents, phone toll-free (866) 512-1800.

OSHA Publications

OSHA has an extensive publications program. For a listing of free or sales items, visit OSHA's website at www.osha.gov or contact the OSHA Publications Office, U.S. Department of Labor, 200 Constitution Avenue, NW, N-3101, Washington, DC 20210. Telephone (202) 693-1888 or fax to (202) 693-2498.

Contacting OSHA

To report an emergency, file a complaint or seek OSHA advice, assistance or products, call (800) 321-OSHA or contact your nearest OSHA regional or area office listed at the end of this publication. The teletypewriter (TTY) number is (877) 889-5627.

You can also file a complaint online and obtain more information on OSHA Federal and state programs by visiting OSHA's website at www.osha.gov

OSHA Regional Offices

Region I
(CT,* ME, MA, NH, RI, VT*)
JFK Federal Building, Room E340
Boston, MA 02203
(617) 565-9860

Region II
(NJ,* NY,* PR,* VI*)
201 Varick Street, Room 670
New York, NY 10014
(212) 337-2378

Region III
(DE, DC, MD,* PA, VA,* WV)
The Curtis Center
170 S. Independence Mall West
Suite 740 West
Philadelphia, PA 19106-3309
(215) 861-4900

Region IV
(AL, FL, GA, KY,* MS, NC,* SC,* TN*)
61 Forsyth Street, SW
Atlanta, GA 30303
(404) 562-2300

Region V
(IL, IN,* MI,* MN,* OH, WI)
230 South Dearborn Street
Room 3244
Chicago, IL 60604
(312) 353-2220

Region VI
(AR, LA, NM,* OK, TX)
525 Griffin Street, Room 602
Dallas, TX 75202
(214) 767-4731 or 4736 x224

Region VII
(IA,* KS, MO, NE)
City Center Square
1100 Main Street, Suite 800
Kansas City, MO 64105
(816) 426-5861

Region VIII
(CO, MT, ND, SD, UT,* WY*)
1999 Broadway, Suite 1690
PO Box 46550
Denver, CO 80202-5716
(720) 264-6550

Region IX
(American Samoa, AZ,* CA,* HI,* NV,*
Northern Mariana Islands)
71 Stevenson Street, Room 420
San Francisco, CA 94105
(415) 975-4310

Region X
(AK,* ID, OR,* WA*)
1111 Third Avenue, Suite 715
Seattle, WA 98101-3212
(206) 553-5930

* These states and territories operate their own OSHA-approved job safety and health programs (Connecticut, New Jersey, New York and the Virgin Islands plans cover public employees only). States with approved programs must have standards that are identical to, or at least as effective as, the Federal standards.

Note: To get contact information for OSHA Area Offices, OSHA-approved State Plans and OSHA Consultation Projects, please visit us online at www.osha.gov or call us at 1-800-321-OSHA.

www.ingramcontent.com/pod-product-compliance
Lightning Source LLC
Chambersburg PA
CBHW071544170526
45166CB00004B/1548